¡Muchas Gracias María!

Written by
Luke Lowenfield

Illustrated by
Hal Marcus

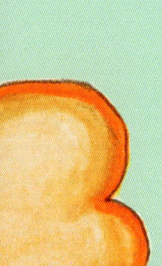

¡Muchas Gracias María!
First Edition, 2020

Text © by Luke Lowenfield, 2020 • Lowenfield.com
Artwork © by Hal Marcus, 2020 • HalMarcus.com
Design by Jud Burgess ⁄ Substance • JudBurgess.com

Published by Paso al Sol
1319 N. Oregon
El Paso, TX 79902
(915) 920-8133
halmarcus123@gmail.com

Library of Congress Control Number: 2020914181

ISBN # 978-0-578-68941-8

A child celebrates his birthday with the love and support of his grandmother from Mexico.

No part of this publication may be reproduced in any form without prior written permission from the author and illustrator.

Printed in PRC

A very special thanks to the Junior League of El Paso for their community support.

Hal Marcus Gallery
1308 N. Oregon
El Paso, Texas 79902
(915) 533-9090
halmarcus.com

El Paso Strong

Dedicated to all the "Marías" who have cared for us from generation to generation.

I smile when I see Abuela María waiting at school for me.
Outside, she takes me by the hand,
and I feel light and free.

When I'm with her
the air around me seems to get soft and warm,
like a peaceful desert morning after a nighttime thunderstorm.

Together we make a cake and tamales.
She teaches me a song.
"Estas son las mañanitas,"
I try to sing along.

Mom and Dad help me learn more Spanish like *gracias, por favor* and *de nada*. They teach me that life on the border is special because we get the whole enchilada.

"Wake up, my love," I hear Mom whisper, "we have exciting news."
"We're going to visit María this morning.
There's a gift in Juárez for you!"

Inside Abuela María's house,
	I don't believe what I see—

a star-shaped piñata,
	dancing in rainbows,
		three times the size of me!

María can tell that my birthday piñata is
too big to fit in our car.

She asks her neighbor to borrow his truck,
and together we all lift the star.

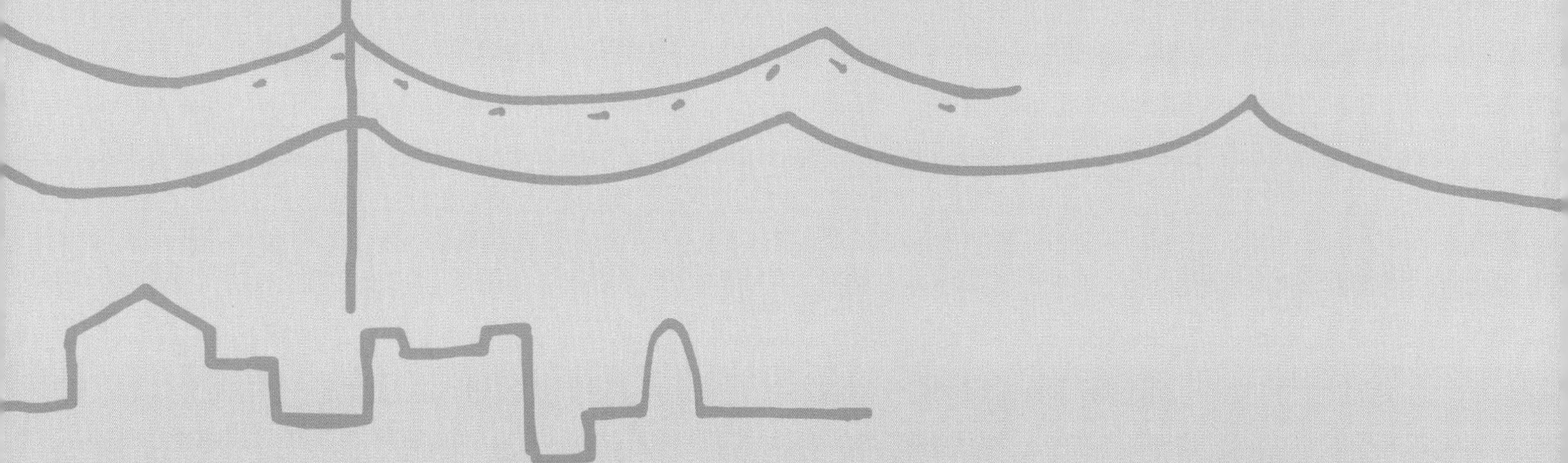

A woman with flowers waves while we drive
down the festive and loud, crowded streets.

"Dios te bendiga," María replies.
She blesses whoever she meets.

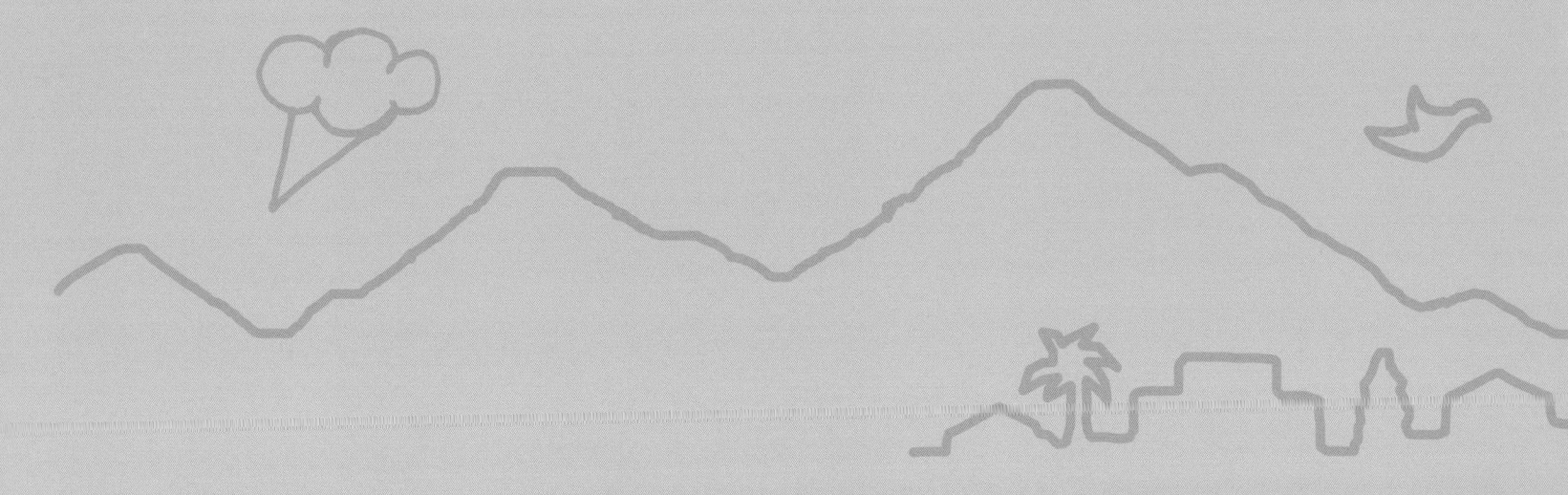

When we get to the park it's just like my daydream,
  with family and friends waiting there,
but now I wonder how we will get my piñata up in the air.

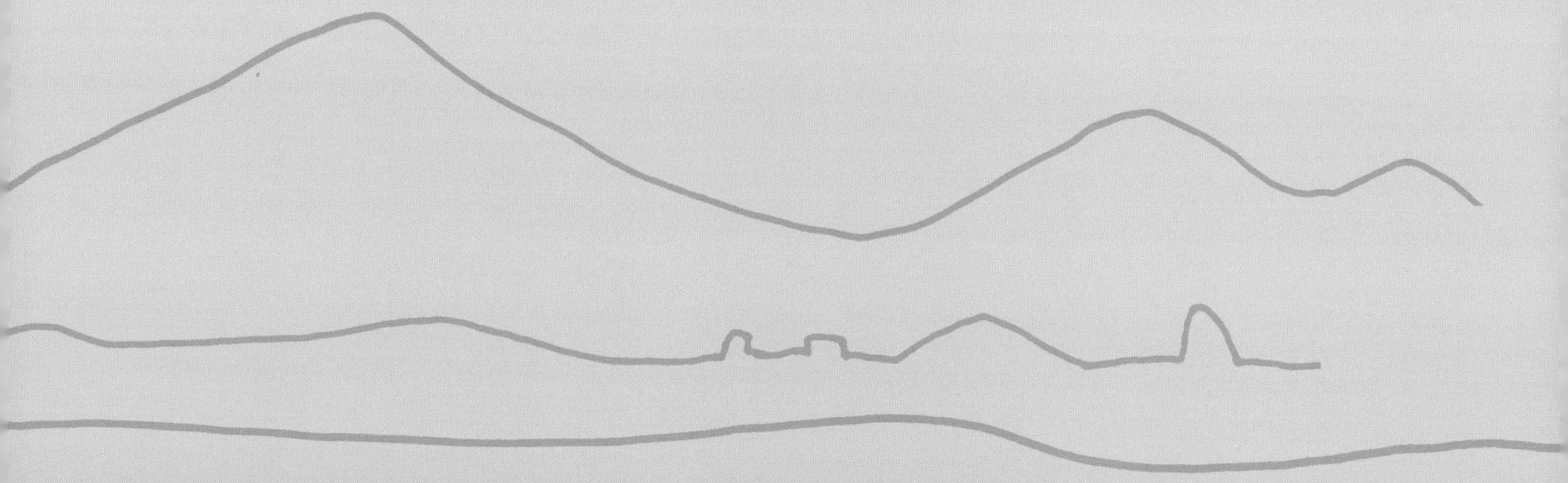

"No worries," I hear María say as she leads us toward a tree.

"I'll climb to the top, and the star will lift off. I've done this before, you'll see."

We all take three swings, the piñata breaks open, and the candies finally fly free. I'll always remember María that way, smiling with pride over me.

Luke Lowenfield's hometown experience, like most El Pasoans, was shaped by generations of family and two languages. El Paso's Hispanic heritage makes the city one of the warmest, most welcoming places in America. Luke's grandmother, Patricia, was born in Tampico, and her family moved to Texas when she was a child. She settled in El Paso after attending Texas Western, where she met her husband, Wally. Luke is blessed to have grandparents like Pat and Wally, and, on his mom's side, Doris and Ron, who have loved and guided him throughout life.

Luke is also the author of *Buenas Noches El Paso*, a story about dreams becoming reality for a child in the beautiful borderland. He studied Spanish Literature at Washington & Lee University, Children's Literature at Pennsylvania State University, and received his law degree from the University of Texas. His wife, Stacey, and children, Parker and Jackson, are his greatest joys.

Hal Marcus has been a professional artist for 50 years. He is a gallery owner, art collector, and publisher. His artwork is best known for depicting El Paso's unique borderland culture, and it has been exhibited in museums and private collections worldwide.

He and his wife, Patricia, live in the historic Sunset Heights neighborhood in a 100-year-old home. Across the street is the Hal Marcus Gallery, which was established in 1996 and represents hundreds of local artists. Marcus has three children, Leilainia, Marco, and Adelaide, who have professionally developed their gifts in the arts, as well.

In 1976, Marcus founded *Paso al Sol* to publish fine art prints, cards, calendars and books. *Muchas Gracias María* is his ninth book and his fourth children's book. Marcus is proud to announce his release of *Aunt Alice Alligator's Animal Alphabet Album*. This stunning, second-edition collectors' publication is now available in hardback.

Canción de la Piñata

Dale, dale, dale,
No pierdas el tino,
Porque si lo pierdes
Pierdes el camino.

Dale, dale, dale,
No pierdas el tino,
Mide la distancia
Que hay en el camino.

Ya le diste una,
Ya le diste dos,
Ya le diste tres
Y tu tiempo se acabó.